heal

Germany

Germany

By Jean F. Blashfield

Enchantment of the World™
Second Series

Children's Press®

An Imprint of Scholastic Inc.

New York Toronto London Auckland Sydney
Mexico City New Delhi Hong Kong
Danbury, Connecticut

Frontispiece: Old timbered house, Celle, Lower Saxony

Consultant: Harold James, Professor of History and International Affairs, Princeton University, Princeton, New Jersey

Please note: All statistics are as up-to-date as possible at the time of publication.

Book production by The Design Lab

Library of Congress Cataloging-in-Publication Data

Blashfield, Jean F.
  Germany / by Jean F. Blashfield.
      pages cm. — (Enchantment of the world. Second series)
  Includes bibliographical references and index.
  ISBN 978-0-531-25601-5 (lib. bdg. : alkaline paper)
  1. Germany—Juvenile literature. I. Title.
  DD17.B532 2013
  943—dc23   2012047068

1 2 3 4 5 6 7 8 9 10 R 22 21 20 19 18 17 16 15 14 13

Germany

Contents

Cover photo:
Neuschwanstein
Castle

Jasmund National Park

White-tailed eagle

At the Heart of Europe

8

THE NATION OF GERMANY LIES AT THE HEART OF Europe. It is at Europe's heart geographically because it is located in central Europe. It is at Europe's heart historically because over the centuries it has often controlled other nations around it. It is at Europe's heart culturally because it has produced many great scientists, artists, writers, composers, and philosophers who influenced the world. And now it lies at the center of Europe economically because it is the strongest nation of the twenty-seven nations that make up the European Union (EU). Germany will play a central role in determining the future of the EU.

Opposite: **In Germany, many green valleys sit in the shadow of towering gray mountain peaks.**

Looking Back

The name Germany dates back to the time when the ancient Romans ruled much of Europe. They referred to the tribal people who lived far to the north and east of Italy as the

GERMANY

- Cities of over 500,000 people
- Other cities
- National capital

0   80 miles

0   120 kilometers

DENMARK

Baltic Sea

North Sea

Heligoland Bight

Schleswig-Holstein

Kiel Canal

Hiddensee I.

Jasmund Natl. Park

Fehmarn I.

Kiel

Rügen I.

Lübeck

Rostock

Hamburg

Lauenburg Lakes Nature Reserve

Müritz Natl. Park

Bremerhaven

Elbe R.

Lake Müritz

Oldenburg

Bremen

Lower Oder Valley Natl. Park

NETHERLANDS

Weser R.

Aller R.

Former division of East and West Germany

POLAND

Osnabrück

Hanover

Brunswick

Berlin

Münster

Hildesheim

Magdeburg

Potsdam

Hamm

Paderborn

Harz Natl. Park

Oberhausen

Dortmund

Göttingen

Halle

Cottbus

Düsseldorf

Essen

Kassel

Leipzig

Saxon Switzerland Natl. Park

Neuss

Wuppertal

Rhine R.

Cologne

Kellerwald-Edersee Natl. Park

Hainich Natl. Park

Dresden

Aachen

Drachenfels Nature Reserve

Erfurt

Jena

Chemnitz

Bonn

Werra R.

Eifel Natl. Park

Koblenz

Mosel R.

Frankfurt

Mainz

Main R.

Würzburg

N

W   E

S

CZECH REPUBLIC

Mannheim

Nuremberg

LUX.

Saarbrücken

Heilbronn

Bavarian Forest Natl. Park

Rhine R.

Regensburg

Danube R.

FRANCE

Stuttgart

Ulm

Danube R.

Ingolstadt

Isar R.

Augsburg

Lake Constance

Munich

AUSTRIA

Berchtesgaden Natl. Park

SWITZERLAND

ITALY

Germany

Germani. No one knows the original meaning of the word. Perhaps it was the name of a specific tribe.

Many tribal people moved through the area, settled, and often moved on again. They became known as the Germanic people. The people who spoke a common language came to be called the *deutsch*, meaning "the people." That separated them from the higher-ups in the church and government who spoke Latin. Eventually, they called their land Deutschland. And that is what the Germans call their country today.

Fields of brilliantly colored tulips brighten the landscape in central Germany.

Just as the United States was formed by thirteen separate colonies coming together, today's Germany was formed from many separate small kingdoms, principalities, and duchies (which had dukes as their leaders). These places joined as a single nation, the German Empire, in 1871. Even today, most Germans look back on their ancestry and call themselves Bavarians, Saxons, or Brandenburgians, the way Americans might say they're Texans, Californians, Michiganders. Twenty-seven different states formed the German Empire. By the time modern Germany was formed as East Germany and West Germany in 1949, many of the states had combined, so there were only sixteen states.

In Bavaria, the traditional folk outfit includes short leather pants called lederhosen.

Twice in the twentieth century, Germany became very powerful and tried to take over other European countries. Each time, after devastating wars that cost the lives of tens of millions of people, it was defeated by an alliance of other European nations and the United States.

People exit the main train station in Frankfurt, one of Germany's largest cities. Today, Frankfurt is thriving, as is Germany as a whole.

Working Together

Today, Germany is the powerhouse of the European Union. But some Germans don't want their country to be so powerful. They remember the terrible things that happened in the twentieth century. Not even Angela Merkel, Germany's chancellor, or leader, since 2005, wants Germany to stand out from the other countries. She wants Germany to be part of a European Union that pulls together for the good of all of its member nations. She has said, "Europe only succeeds if we work together." That "if" will affect the future of both Europe and the world.

Land of Rivers and Mountains

ERMANY IS A LAND OF GRAND RIVERS AND MAJESTIC mountains. The nation stretches across central Europe, covering an area of 137,846 square miles (357,000 square kilometers). That is a little smaller than the U.S. state of Montana. Germany is bordered by nine other nations, more than any other nation in Europe. They are Poland, the Czech Republic, Austria, Switzerland, France, Luxembourg, Belgium, the Netherlands, and Denmark. Its longest border is with Austria, and it winds for 487 miles (784 km).

Opposite: **The Rhine River cuts through western Germany on its way to the North Sea.**

Northern Islands

Germany has 1,484 miles (2,388 km) of coastline along the North Sea and the Baltic Sea. Several islands in these seas belong to Germany, including some of the Frisian Islands, a long chain of islands in the North Sea along the northern coast of Germany and the Netherlands and the west coast of Denmark. Farther away from the mainland is a large island called Helgoland.

The soft white chalk cliffs at Jasmund National Park are constantly wearing away. During each storm that hits, parts of the cliffs fall into the sea.

Germany's largest island, Rügen, lies in the Baltic Sea. It can be reached from the mainland by road and railway. Much of the island is protected as Jasmund National Park, Germany's smallest national park. Jasmund features spectacular chalk cliffs, which soar up to 528 feet (161 meters) high, and much of the park is covered in beech forests.

The Lost City

In 1362, a storm caused high waves that washed away the city of Rungholt on the island of Strand in the North Sea. The city was rebuilt, but three centuries later it disappeared again in the same kind of storm. This time, the people of Rungholt did not rebuild. Legend has it that church bells from the city can still be heard ringing underwater. Some people think that the lost city itself is a legend, but remnants of it sometimes wash ashore.

The Northern Lowlands

A lowland area lies along Germany's northern coast, near the North Sea and the Baltic Sea. Areas along the North Sea are so low-lying that people have built dikes, or long walls, to keep the sea from flooding the land during storm surges, when wind forces the water up over the land. The first dikes in the area were constructed at least a thousand years ago. Today, some dikes are almost 29 feet (9 m) high.

The North German Plain covers most of the northern part of the country. A fairly flat area, it never rises higher than about 650 feet (200 m). It was probably once a great forest, but today much of it is farmland. Rivers and canals crisscross the land.

Lake of Konstanz
538 square Km

Lake Müritz is the largest lake entirely within Germany. It spreads across 44 square miles (114 sq km).

The plain in northeastern Germany features lakes and wetlands. The Mecklenburg Lake District, also in that area, lies in Müritz National Park. More than a hundred lakes are scattered across the park, including Lake Müritz, the largest lake entirely within Germany's borders.

Germany's historic industrial center also lies in the North German Plain. Coal underlying the area reaches the surface near the Ruhr River. This coal provided the power that made the region the production center for iron and steel in the early 1900s. The iron and steel industry in the Ruhr Valley allowed Germany to become an industrial powerhouse. Coal is no longer mined along the Ruhr today, and the land has been replanted as parkland.

Many small villages are nestled in the forests in the Harz Mountains.

Germany's Geographic Features

Area: 137,846 square miles (357,000 sq km)

Greatest Distance North to South: 540 miles (870 km)

Greatest Distance East to West: 390 miles (628 km)

Highest Elevation: Zugspitze (above), 9,717 feet (2,962 m) above sea level

Lowest Elevation: In Neuendorf bei Wilster, Schleswig-Holstein, 11.6 feet (3.5 m) below sea level

Longest River: Rhine, 542 miles (872 km) in Germany, 766 miles (1,233 km) total

Average High Temperature: In Berlin, 75°F (24°C) in July; 37°F (3°C) in January

Average Annual Precipitation: 20 to 28 inches (51 to 71 cm) in the northern lowlands; 80 inches (203 cm) in the Bavarian Alps

Highest Recorded Temperature: 104.4°F (40.2°C) at Karlsruhe on August 13, 2003

Lowest Recorded Temperature: −50.6°F (−45.9°C) at Berchtesgaden National Park on December 24, 2001

A skier races down a ski slope on the Zugspitze.

Central Germany

In the Central German Uplands, the land starts to rise toward the southern Alps. In this area, higher forested land lies next to open farmland. The Germans call such land *Mittelgebirge*, which means "low mountain range."

The highest spots in the Central German Uplands lie in the Harz Mountains. The highest peak is Brockenberg, which reaches to 3,747 feet (1,142 m).

Between the Central Uplands and the mountains of southern Germany is a region called Alpine Foreland. It starts at the Danube River and rises toward the foothills of the Alps. This is mostly rough land scoured by the glaciers that once covered the area. Munich is the most important city in the region.

The Bavarian Alps

South of the Central German Uplands, the land rises fairly quickly toward the Alps, towering mountains that boast Europe's highest peaks. The Alps are divided into a series of ranges, including the Bavarian Alps in Germany.

Germany's highest peak is the Zugspitze, at 9,717 feet (2,962 m). This peak rises above the ski resort area of Garmisch-Partenkirchen, on the border with Austria. Three cable cars carry skiers up the mountain.

Between the peaks of the Alps are lush valleys. Winding through them is the German Alpine Road. It runs for 280 miles (450 km) through long tunnels and past bright blue lakes, hilltop castles, and stunning peaks.

The Rhine River Valley

High in the Alps lies Lake Constance, the third-largest lake in Europe. Long ago, ancient glaciers gouged out this lake, which straddles the border where Germany, Austria, and Switzerland meet. Germany's main river, the Rhine, flows west from the lake,

Stories from the Rhine

German composer Richard Wagner wrote a series of operas called *The Ring of the Nibelung*, which tells the stories of Norse gods. The first opera in the series, *Das Rheingold* ("The Rhine Gold"), introduces three Rhine maidens who guard gold in the river. A dwarf steals the gold, makes it into a ring, and thus begins the long saga. Tourists traveling the Rhine River are told that the maidens lived in the area around the Rhine Gorge.

forming the boundary between Germany and Switzerland. Near Basel, Switzerland, it turns northward, where it forms the border with France. The Rhine flows for a total of 766 miles (1,233 km). More than two-thirds of that length is within Germany.

One of the outstanding stretches of the river is the Rhine Gorge, or the Upper Middle Rhine Valley. Between the cities of Bingen and Bonn, forty romantic castles perch on high cliffs overlooking the river.

Several large rivers feed into the Rhine. The Mosel flows into it from France. The two rivers meet at Koblenz. The Main River flows across Germany and meets the Rhine at Wiesbaden. The Neckar flows northward from the Black Forest, meeting the Rhine at Mannheim.

Many locks on the Rhine raise and lower the level of the river. This allows large cargo ships to travel stretches of the river they would otherwise not be able to.

The Danube, another major river in Germany, begins in the Black Forest in the southwestern part of the country. It

Cleaning up the Rhine

In 1986, a fire in a factory in Switzerland sent tons of red-colored poisonous chemicals into the Rhine River. The polluting chemicals flowed northward, turning the river red and damaging the nearby land. The chemicals killed life in the river and even wiped out some species completely. The countries the river flows through started the Rhine Action Program (RAP) to clean up the pollution. The river is now clean enough for wildlife, including salmon, to return. Swimmers, too, can enjoy the water.

then flows for 1,785 miles (2,873 km), touching ten countries, before emptying into the Black Sea at the southwestern
edge of Europe. In 1992, a canal that connects the Rhine, the
Main, and the Danube was completed. It allows ships to travel
all the way from the North Sea to the Black Sea.

A barge travels down the Danube River in southern Germany. The second-longest river in Europe, the Danube touches ten countries.

Climate

In most of Germany, the weather is determined by the masses
of air that flow across Europe from the east. These air masses are
generally quite warm in summer and cold in winter. One unusual
element is that it is warmer in the north than in the south.

Summer temperatures in low-lying regions average 64
degrees Fahrenheit (17.8 degrees Celsius), and in alpine valleys 68°F (20°C). July is the rainiest time across the country,
so the skies are more likely to be cloudy than sunny.

Winter temperatures tend to be warmer if an air mass is coming from the Atlantic and colder if the air is coming from the east. Low-lying areas have winter temperatures averaging 35°F (1.6°C), while the mountains average 21°F (–6°C).

In the autumn, mountainous regions sometimes experience the foehn, a dry wind that comes from the east, bringing beautiful clear skies and pleasantly cool temperatures. These winds can come on suddenly, abruptly raising the temperature, surprising skiers by how quickly the snow melts under their skis.

In autumn, Germany's forests turn brilliant shades of yellow and orange.

Germany's Biggest Cities

Berlin, the capital of Germany, is the nation's biggest city by far with a population of about 3.4 million. With a population of close to 1.8 million, Hamburg is Germany's second-largest city. Located on the Elbe River near the North Sea, it is also the nation's most important port (right). Hamburg is a center of publishing and broadcasting. It has many theaters, concert halls, and clubs, creating a thriving cultural life. The world's largest model railway museum is just one of many museums in this city.

The nation's third-largest city is Munich (below), with 1.2 million people. Now the capital of Bavaria in southern Germany, it was founded around 1158 CE on the site of a monastery. The name *Munich* means "monk settlement." Today, Munich is a center of high-

tech and media industries. Its annual Oktoberfest draws visitors from all over the world.

The jewel of the Rhine River valley is Cologne, Germany's fourth-largest city, with just about 1 million people. The ancient Romans settled this city more than two thousand years ago, and Roman ruins are still being found there. The city boasts a magnificent cathedral and a lively cultural scene. Like Hamburg, Cologne has many media businesses.

Frankfurt lies on the Main River. Though the city itself has only about 700,000 people, it is the center of Germany's largest urban area after Berlin. The city's very modern skyline stands in stark contrast to the medieval streets of the city. Frankfurt is the nation's center of finance and the headquarters of the European Central Bank, which controls the euro currency used in much of the European Union. Frankfurt Airport is one of the busiest in the world.

The Natural World

GERMANY IS A LAND OF FORESTS. IT HAS MORE forested land than any other European nation. The Black Forest gets its name from the dark, evergreen fir trees that fill the landscape. The Black Forest also has deciduous trees, which lose their leaves in the winter. Some of these trees, especially walnut, are used to make cuckoo clocks and other carved crafts for which the region is famous.

Beech trees are the most common hardwood trees in central Europe. The Harz Mountains get their name from the German for "wooded land," and that wood is beech. Beechwood is most often used to make half-timbered houses in Germany, which feature exposed wooden beams. The smoke from burning beech also gives a special flavor to some German cheeses.

Opposite: **A wild goat walks through a field at a nature reserve near Cologne.**

Mammals

Many mammals live in the forests of Germany. Wild goats and wild cats thrive there. Red, roe, and fallow deer are all common. Wolves disappeared from Germany 150 years ago. Recently, however, they have begun to move back into Germany from Poland.

The Green Belt

In the decades after World War II, Germany was split into two countries, commonly known as East Germany and West Germany. A narrow strip of land separated the two countries. To stop people from crossing from the east to the west, more than a million land mines were planted along the east-west border, and ditches were dug. Today, this strip of land has become a "green belt" that stretches nearly 870 miles (1,400 km). The strip includes many kinds of habitat, including wetlands, woodlands, and grasslands. Wildlife now thrives there. Otters swim in ditches that had been dug to stop vehicles. An organization called Bund Naturschutz is trying to buy up as much of the land as possible in the green belt in order to protect it.

Many smaller animals also live in Germany. Otters swim in the rivers, and pine martens, which are related to weasels, live in wooded areas. They may venture into towns, where they sometimes chew on the soft parts of cars. Pine martens have a vivid cream or yellowish bib on the throat, which makes them look as if they are wearing bandannas.

Also venturing into populated areas is the much bigger wild boar, often called the Russian boar. An adult male boar, which has tusks, often grows to more than 6 feet (1.8 m) long and weighs more than 200 pounds (90 kilograms).

The European bison, or wisent, went extinct in the wild in 1927. But now, descendants of some captive wisents are being reintroduced into Germany. Wisents are taller than American bison but weigh less.

Some mammals arrived in Germany only recently. The raccoon dog is neither a raccoon nor a dog. A relative of the fox, it is in the dog family, however, and it is striped and masked like a raccoon. Germans imported the creatures from Japan. They wanted to breed the raccoon dogs for their soft, thick fur, but some animals escaped from the fur farms and quickly multiplied. They can climb trees, where they feed on birds, rodents, and amphibians, and they hibernate in winter.

In Europe, raccoon dogs are considered pests because they prey on birds and spread disease.

Dogs and More Dogs

Some of the most popular dog breeds around the world began in Germany. One of the best known is the German shepherd, also known as the Alsatian. This breed was developed in the late 1800s as a herding dog. It was bred for its intelligence, loyalty, and tendency to protect. The Doberman pinscher was bred as a guard dog around 1900. The very tall Great Dane was originally bred to hunt boars. Rottweilers are large husky dogs that were once used like little ponies to pull carts. They now often serve as guide dogs for the blind.

Schnauzers (right), which date back to the Middle Ages, were named for their snouts, or *Schnauze*, because they have prominent beards. They come in three varieties: giant, standard, and miniature. Poodles also come in multiple sizes. Though originally working dogs, poodles are now favored as indoor pets.

Birds

More than five hundred species of birds are seen in Germany. Some live there year-round, while others pass through on their yearly migration. Still others breed in Germany and then go on their way to other locations.

Storks are among the largest birds that live in Germany. White storks have white bodies, black wing feathers, and bright red bills and legs. Their legs are long and their wingspan stretches up to 7 feet (2 m). When storks are born, their beaks are black, but then gradually turn red as the birds grow up. White storks winter in Africa but return to Europe to lay eggs and raise their young. Germans sometimes put flat platforms on the roofs of their houses to attract storks to nest there, which is considered good luck.

The slightly smaller and shyer black stork lives in some forested areas of eastern Germany. This bird winters in Africa and India, and then flies north for the summer.

Other large birds in Germany include the common crane, which migrates across Germany between Scandinavia, in northern Europe, and North Africa. Thousands of these gray cranes

Adult common cranes have a white stripe and red splotch on their heads. Young cranes lack this coloring.

The National Bird

Germany's national bird is the white-tailed eagle, which is closely related to the bald eagle. It is a very large bird, with a wingspan that can reach 8 feet (2.4 m). White-tailed eagles almost became extinct because farmers and gamekeepers, wrongly thinking the eagles preyed on farm animals, tried to get rid of them. In fact, the eagles' diet is mainly fish, other birds, and small mammals. They are also scavengers, eating whatever dead animals they find. White-tailed eagles have been protected in Germany since 1970.

sometimes roost in one location at a time, making a stunning sight. Common cranes have loud, honking calls and elaborate courtship dances. The smaller demoiselle crane is also gray in color. It is less common in Germany than its larger relative.

Cuckoos have some of the most recognizable calls of all birds. Their familiar call is reproduced in the cuckoo clocks that have been made in the Black Forest for centuries. Cuckoos often lay their eggs in the nests of other birds, especially warblers and pipits. The other birds tend to the eggs until they hatch.

Northern Germany has many wetlands, including river estuaries, where freshwater and saltwater mix. Wetlands attract migrating birds, especially waders such as herons and egrets.

The common cuckoo spends summers in Europe and Asia and winters in Africa. It feeds mostly on insects.

Hedges grow between many of the fields and meadows on the North German Plain. These have become home to many smaller birds, such as sparrows. Hawks, vultures, and buzzards fly overhead. In the cities, wrens, pigeons, thrushes, and crows are common.

Visitors explore ruins at Drachenfels. The name means "dragon's rock."

National Parks

Germany has created many national parks and reserves to protect its diverse landscapes and the plants and animals that live there. Drachenfels, near Cologne, was protected in 1836, making it what is considered today to be the world's first nature reserve. Drachenfels was formed through ancient volcanic activity. The rough rocks on the top of the hill bear the remains of a fortress built at least a thousand years ago.

The steep cliffs at Saxon Switzerland National Park make it popular with rock climbers.

Germany's first national park was Bavarian Forest National Park, established in 1970. While many German forests were being cut down and built over, this forest was left alone to grow. The forest houses a variety of owls, including the rare pygmy owl.

The newest of Germany's fourteen national parks is Eifel, near Cologne, which was established in 2004. It protects more than 230 endangered animal and plant species.

The parks cover a wide variety of landscapes. Saxon Switzerland in the eastern part of the country near the Czech border features a rocky landscape that has been called the "Grand Canyon of Germany." Hainich National Park has oak trees that are a thousand years old. It also features the

Wildcat Children's Forest, which has an elevated walkway high up in the treetops, giving hikers a view of the top of the forest. Red deer, ospreys, cranes, and black storks draw visitors to the Müritz National Park in northeastern Germany. Berchtesgaden National Park is a highlight of the Bavarian Alps. It includes three valleys and many peaks, including Mount Watzmann, Germany's third-highest mountain.

Germany shares Lower Oder Valley National Park with Poland. This park features meadowlands on the banks of the river. Beavers and otters live in the waters, and many migratory birds stop there. Western Pomerania Lagoon Area National Park on the Baltic Sea consists mainly of bodden, which are shallow bays mostly enclosed by land. Many species of birds nest along the bodden or stop by on their migration.

The Biggest Zoo

Germany has more zoos than the United States. At least 414 animal parks are registered as zoos. The country also has many specialized animal parks, such as butterfly farms and reptile parks.

The Berlin Zoo, located in the huge park called the Tiergarten, is one of the largest zoos in the world. More than 17,000 animals representing over 1,500 species live there. The zoo originally opened in 1844, but was totally destroyed during World War II. Only about ninety of the thousands of animals housed there survived the war. When the zoo was rebuilt after the war, it was completely redesigned to give the animals more natural habitats. Now, the penguins live on real ice and snow, and the hippopotamuses have large ponds to swim in.

A Tangled History

AFTER THE LAST ICE AGE ENDED ABOUT TEN thousand years ago, various tribes of people from the east ventured into the land now known as Germany. One of the earliest groups was the Celts, who gradually spread across Europe. One group of Celts called the Gauls invaded ancient Rome from the north several times. Roman general Julius Caesar invaded Gaul beginning in 58 BCE. Caesar built the first bridge across the Rhine River, though he later removed it so that the tribal warriors could not cross. Later Roman forces also attacked the people who lived farther away than the Celts. Writers in ancient Rome called all the various tribes of people to their north the Germani. Experts are unsure what it meant. It might have been the name of a certain tribe.

Opposite: **In 9 CE, German tribes defeated the Roman army at the Battle of the Teutoburg Forest in what is now northwestern Germany.**

The Holy Roman Empire

After about 500 CE, the Roman Empire lost its might, and a Germanic tribe called the Franks became the most powerful group in the region. Their primary leader was Charlemagne (Charles the Great). He was a Christian who wanted to

Charlemagne ruled for almost fifty years.

impose Christianity on all the tribes. Gradually, he brought them all under his control. After he extended his power into Italy, the pope—the leader of the Roman Catholic Church—crowned him emperor in 800 CE.

Charlemagne decreed that Latin, the language of the church, would be the official language of his empire. After his death in 814, his empire split up as various leaders fought to take his place. The language spoken in the western part of the empire, based on Latin, became French. The language used in the eastern part became German.

The German-speaking region became the Holy Roman Empire, which lasted from 962 to 1806. It extended through what are now Belgium and Luxembourg, along with parts of France and Italy. The Holy Roman Empire included many small countries, some controlled by dukes, some by princes, and some by kings. These individual states were never linked together strongly, so it was an empire in name only. The French writer Voltaire once said, "The Holy Roman Empire was neither holy, nor Roman, nor an empire."

The Reformation

The Germanic states in the Holy Roman Empire were Catholic. But one monk named Martin Luther objected to the way the Roman Catholic Church let people buy "forgiveness" for sins by paying money to the church. These payments were called indulgences. In 1517, Luther posted on a church door in Wittenberg a list of objections called *The Ninety-Five Theses*. It contained all the things the church did that he believed were in opposition to the Bible. This started a period called the Reformation, because Luther and the other founders of the new Protestant groups believed they were "reforming" the Roman Catholic Church.

The development of Protestantism helped drive the Germanic states apart. Some of the states insisted on remaining within the Roman Catholic Church. Others became Protestant. The two sides fought against each other during the Thirty Years' War,

The Hanseatic League

Northern Germany along the coasts of the North Sea and the Baltic Sea was once part of a huge trading group called the Hanseatic League, or the Hansa. From the thirteenth to the seventeenth century, this business alliance was the only official trader in that region. The league's trade and armies reached north into Scandinavia, east into Russia, and west into England. Reminders of the league still exist. The German national airline, for example, is called Lufthansa, meaning "air of the Hansa." Some cities, such as Hamburg and Lübeck, are still officially "Free Hanseatic Cities," which indicate that they were once part of the league.

which lasted from 1618 to 1648. The war impoverished various states in the Holy Roman Empire, but by the time peace was declared, each state was able to choose its own religion.

Two families played a central role in Germany during the following years. The Habsburgs, who ruled the Holy Roman Empire for many years, led the kingdoms that became the Austro-Hungarian Empire. The Hohenzollerns developed the Kingdom of Prussia into a great power. The Prussians had a well-organized army, which they used to expand their

The Thirty Years' War was devastating to Europe. The armies scoured the land for food, often leaving the local people to starve. More than a quarter of the German population died during the war.

territory. King Frederick the Great united several areas of Germany and modernized the army and government of Prussia.

Napoléon's Empire

At the end of the eighteenth century, General Napoléon Bonaparte came to power in France. He was soon engaged in wars all across Europe. In the process, he took over large parts of Germany. The rulers of small kingdoms quickly agreed to his demands. Other kingdoms fought against Napoléon's armies. After losing to Napoléon in the 1805 Battle of Austerlitz in what is now the Czech Republic, Francis II, the head of the Holy Roman Empire, declared that the empire no longer existed. Instead, he formed the Austrian Empire and became its first emperor.

Frederick the Great was a brilliant military commander. He greatly increased Prussia's power.

Napoléon sent his army of almost half a million men to Russia in 1812. By December 1812, Prussian forces had joined the Russians to fight Napoléon. The Russian winter and the combination of Russian and Prussian troops were too powerful for Napoléon's army. Hundreds of thousands of soldiers died. Napoléon gave up and returned to France. He was finally

The Mad King

Bavarian King Ludwig II was only eighteen years old when he came to the throne in 1864. He wasn't very good at being king. In fact, he wasn't king for very long because Prussia soon captured Bavaria. So the young king concentrated on building beautiful residences. The most enchanting is Neuschwanstein, which sits on a mountaintop in southwestern Bavaria. Ludwig lived in the castle for only a short time. In 1886, after almost bankrupting the state, he was declared insane. He soon drowned in a lake at another of his castles. Did he take his own life or was he murdered? No one knows. Only seven weeks later, Neuschwanstein was opened as a tourist attraction. It also served as the inspiration for Sleeping Beauty's castle at Disneyland.

Central Europe, 1815

☐ German Confederation   ── Present-day Germany

forced to give up power in 1814. The following year, he tried to return from exile and take over again, but strong Prussian forces along with troops from several other nations stopped him in the Battle of Waterloo, in Belgium.

In 1815, the meeting of nations, called the Congress of Vienna, decided what would happen to Europe now that Napoléon had been conquered. The congress gathered thirty-nine different kingdoms and principalities into the German Confederation. But the two most powerful states, the Kingdom of Prussia and the Austrian Empire, continued to compete with each other. The German Confederation faded away by 1866, when the two nations went to war. Prussia was victorious. The Prussian king, Wilhelm I, became the emperor, or kaiser, of the new German Empire.

World War I

By the early twentieth century, countries across Europe were vying for power around the globe. Tensions were running high. War erupted when Archduke Franz Ferdinand, the heir to the throne of Austria, was assassinated in June 1914. Germany, the Austro-Hungarian Empire, and the Ottoman Empire led the Central Powers. They fought the Allies, which consisted of Great Britain, Russia, France, and other countries, and eventually the United States.

Wilhelm I was a soldier and diplomat before becoming the first leader of the German Empire.

World War I lasted for four years, and it was one of the bloodiest conflicts in history. More than ten million soldiers were killed, including almost two million Germans. The Allies set about making Germany pay for the devastation the continent suffered. They drew up the Treaty of Versailles, which took land, including important coalfields and overseas colonies, away from Germany. The treaty shrank Germany's army and

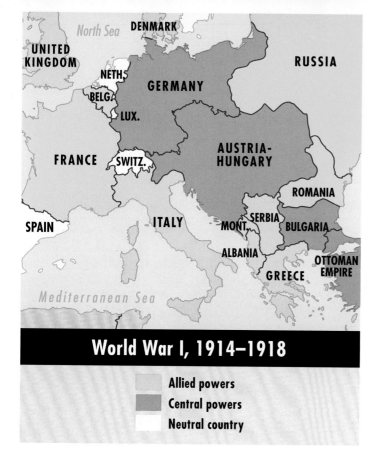

World War I, 1914–1918

Allied powers
Central powers
Neutral country

took away its tanks and air force. It also forced Germany to pay for the damage done to France and Belgium. The new government in Germany, called the Weimar Republic, had little power.

Germany suffered under the treaty. Year by year, conditions became harder for the German people. The economy was so bad that the currency became practically worthless. It took a bagful of German banknotes to buy a single loaf of bread. The anger of the German people grew.

The Rise of Hitler

A new political leader, Adolf Hitler, began to tell the people that life could be better. The German people listened. They listened when he told them that their problems were caused by the Jews, the disabled, the Gypsies, and other people he claimed were "lesser." Jews began to flee from Germany, including scientists such as Albert Einstein.

In 1933, enough members of Hitler's party were elected to make him chancellor, the head of the national government. He took the title of *Führer* ("leader") of the new government he called the Third Reich. (The First Reich was the Holy Roman Empire, and the Second Reich was the German

Empire.) He turned many of his followers into a brutal army that began rounding up political enemies and others he considered "undesirables."

Inflation spiraled out of control in the 1920s in Germany, making money practically worthless. Here, a woman lights her stove with German bills.

Germans backed him in part because he started major projects such as building roads and producing military equipment. He put people to work designing and building automobiles, including the Volkswagen, the "people's car." The nation's economy began to improve as millions of Germans entered the army and millions more got jobs in factories.

As Germany's economy improved, Hitler began building camps, where Jews and the other groups of people he blamed

Volkswagen began operation in 1937. It was founded by the German Labor Front, a Nazi organization.

for Germany's woes were at first detained and then killed. Other nations looked on uneasily as Germany rearmed and as the Nazi government talked about the need for additional room for the superior German people. Some people objected when Germany took over Austria, a German-speaking nation, but did nothing about it. When Hitler began to threaten Poland, the leaders of Great Britain and France promised the Poles that they would not

More than three thousand German tanks rolled into Poland during the German invasion of 1939.

let Germany seize it. When German troops invaded Poland on September 1, 1939, Britain and France were forced to make good on their promise.

World War II

Within months, the mighty German army took over many nations in Europe. Hitler assumed that when he reached France, he could easily cross the English Channel and capture Great Britain. But that did not happen. In what came to be called the Battle of Britain, British pilots kept German airplanes from invading. However, German troops bombed Britain throughout the war.

Adolf Hitler

Adolf Hitler began gaining attention in the 1920s. This was a hard time for Germany, after their defeat in World War I, but Hitler refused to give in to the negative feelings many Germans had following the Treaty of Versailles. He thought that Germans were better than other people, and that their difficulties stemmed from the Jewish people.

Hitler was born in 1889 in Braunau am Inn, Austria. Hitler wanted to become an artist but could not make a career of it. He moved to Munich in 1913 and joined the German army during World War I. After the war, unable to find any occupation, he became involved in politics. He joined a small political party, which he

soon began to run. He often gave public speeches, telling his audiences whom to blame for their troubles. He told them that while they suffered, Jews were thriving. His political party became the National Socialist German Workers' Party, known as the Nazi Party.

Hitler was tried for treason after trying to take over the German government in 1923. During the year of his imprisonment, he wrote *Mein Kampf* ("My Struggle"). This book explained his beliefs and his certainty that Germany was destined for great things. After he was released from prison, Hitler slowly gained power until, in 1933, he became chancellor, the most powerful man in Germany. He soon used his position and power to start a war that destroyed large parts of Europe and killed millions of people. However, in the end, the Allies were victorious. When Hitler realized he had lost the war, he killed himself.

German troops did invade the Soviet Union, a large nation made up of what are now Russia and other nearby countries. Hitler thought it might be easy to gain control there. Instead, German troops became bogged down in blockading the city of Leningrad for 872 days. More than twenty million Soviet soldiers and civilians ultimately died in the war.

Almost every nation in the world became involved in World War II. The United States entered the war when Japan, an ally of Germany's, bombed Pearl Harbor in Hawaii in December 1941.

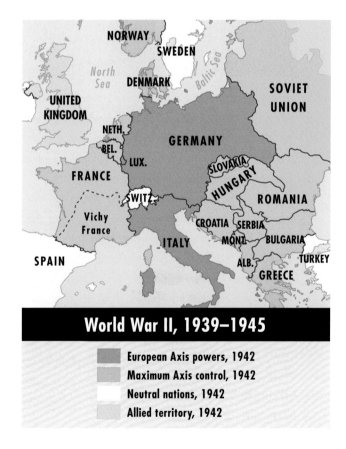

World War II, 1939–1945

- European Axis powers, 1942
- Maximum Axis control, 1942
- Neutral nations, 1942
- Allied territory, 1942

In 1944, the Allies, led by the United States and Great Britain, invaded the European continent and began to push the German armies back. As they entered Germany, they discovered the first of several hundred camps where Jews, Gypsies, the disabled, and others had been imprisoned, starved, worked to death, and deliberately killed. An estimated nine million people, of which six million were Jews, were killed in what became known as the Holocaust.

Hitler, seeing that Germany was losing the war, committed suicide. A devastated Germany surrendered to the Allies on May 8, 1945. The four main Allies—the United States, Great

Britain, France, and the Soviet Union—then occupied Germany. Each took control of one sector, or portion, of Germany.

Jewish children arrive at Auschwitz, one of the thousands of concentration camps the Nazi regime built in Europe during World War II. More than a million people were murdered at Auschwitz.

The Cold War

Very quickly, the alliance among the United States, Great Britain, France, and the Soviet Union ended. The Allies soon became enemies. A battle for power and influence began between Western nations and the Soviet Union. This conflict is called the Cold War. The Western powers, especially the United States, distrusted the Soviet Union because it was a Communist

Devastation

Willy Brandt was the chancellor of West Germany in the early 1970s. He wrote that when World War II ended, Germany was "craters, caves, mountains of rubble, debris-covered fields, ruins that hardly allow one to imagine that they had once been houses, . . . no fuel, no light, every little garden a graveyard and, above all, like an immovable cloud, the stink of putrefaction. In this no man's land lived human beings. Their life was a daily struggle for a handful of potatoes, a loaf of bread, a few lumps of coal."

nation. Under communism, the government owns the businesses and controls the economy. The United States believed that the Soviet Union would spread communism to other nations.

The division of Germany separated families. Here, a mother bids good-bye to her son at the border between the U.S. and Soviet sectors of Germany.

After the war, the Allies set about rebuilding their sectors of Germany. Their three sectors united and wrote a new constitution called the Basic Law. On May 23, 1949, West Germany began as a new nation officially called the German Federal Republic.

The Soviets, on the other hand, wanted to punish Germany and wanted repayment for the damage Germany had done to their land. They removed industry from East Germany, sent it to Russia, and set about turning East Germany into a Communist state. The German Democratic Republic, or East Germany, was established on October 7, 1949.

The United States, meanwhile, had set up the Marshall Plan, which provided money for West Germany and other countries to rebuild. Under this plan, Germany was able to reopen factories and start up businesses. Germany had long had a reputation for making quality goods, and the country was soon a major exporter once again.

Many East Germans envied the economy and freedom of the west. Many fled across the border into West Germany. The easiest place to enter West Germany was in Berlin, where all one had to do was cross a street. Almost two million East Germans soon fled into West Germany.

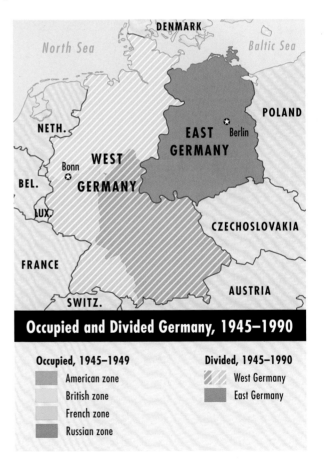

Occupied and Divided Germany, 1945–1990

Occupied, 1945–1949
- American zone
- British zone
- French zone
- Russian zone

Divided, 1945–1990
- West Germany
- East Germany

The Berlin Airlift

The German capital of Berlin lies in the eastern part of Germany, in what was the Soviet sector in the years after World War II. Like the country as a whole, Berlin was also divided into quarters after the war. The Soviet Union controlled one sector, and the Western Allies controlled the other three. The Allies had to bring food and fuel, and everything else Berliners in those three sectors needed, through Soviet-controlled territory. This became an issue in 1948. That year, the Allies in Berlin started using a new currency called the deutsche mark. This angered the Soviets, who wanted to continue to use only the old currency. In response, the Soviets closed off all roads and railroads going into Berlin from the West.

The only way the Allies could supply Berliners with food and fuel was by air. This began the largest aerial supply operation in history. Over the following months, American, British, and French pilots flew more than 270,000 flights into Berlin, carrying more than 2 million tons (1.8 million metric tons) of goods. Less than a year after the airlift started, the Soviet Union again opened ground routes into Berlin. They had accepted that the Allies could continue to supply Berliners by air forever.

The Soviet government could not let the flow of people out of East Germany continue. In 1961, they placed barbed wire across roads and bridges and cut the subway lines. They soon replaced the wire fence with a solid brick wall and guard towers. This was called the Berlin Wall.

Soon after the wall went up, U.S. president John F. Kennedy went to Berlin and spoke to hundreds of thousands of people. He let them know that he supported them in their trials, as he said, *Ich bin ein Berliner*," "I am a Berliner."

In 1972, West Germany let the world know it was thriving by holding the Summer Olympics in Munich. Everything was going according to plan, when members of the Israeli team were captured and held hostage in the Olympic Village. The athletes were taken by the Palestinian group Black September, who wanted Palestinian prisoners in Israeli prisons released. German snipers tried to

About 450,000 people gathered in Berlin to watch U.S. president John F. Kennedy speak.

ambush the kidnappers but failed. A number of other missteps followed, and by the end the Palestinians had killed eleven Israeli athletes and coaches, and one German policeman.

Reunification

Even as West Germany thrived, East Germany and other Eastern European countries dominated by the Soviet Union stagnated. People struggled—sometimes privately, sometimes publicly—for greater freedom. Eventually, change came. In

An East German escaping to the West after climbing over the Berlin Wall. About five thousand people tried to escape over the wall.

1985, a new Soviet leader, Mikhail Gorbachev, took power and began some reforms that gave people greater freedom. In 1987, another American president, Ronald Reagan, came to the Berlin Wall. He challenged the Soviet leader during his speech exclaiming, "Mr. Gorbachev, tear down this wall!"

And it happened. After Communist-controlled Hungary opened its border with Austria, crowds of unhappy East Germans began to demonstrate against their government. The demonstrations grew until November 9, 1989, when the government unexpectedly said that East Germans were free to travel abroad. People eager to leave began massing at the Berlin Wall, which they tore down as the world watched and celebrated. For the first time since 1961, East Berliners were allowed to cross into West Berlin.

People sit atop the Berlin Wall to celebrate its fall in the days after it began to be torn down.

West Germans cheer the stream of East Germans driving across the border on November 9, 1989, the day the border between the two halves of Germany was reopened.

Political power in East Germany fell apart. The Soviet Union soon announced that it approved of the two Germanys reuniting. On October 3, 1990, West and East Germany became one country once again, with its capital at Berlin. A year later, the Soviet Union dissolved, after almost seventy years of existence. The countries that had joined together to form the Soviet Union were once again independent nations.

The New Germany

Since reunification, Germany has become an economic superpower, and currently is the third-largest exporter in the world. It is also the major power in the European Union, a group of twenty-seven nations that work together economically and politically.

Europe began having severe economic problems around 2010. Angela Merkel, the chancellor of Germany, will have to make many important decisions to help solve these problems. Merkel was born in West Germany, raised in East Germany, and now plays a major role in shaping the future of the new Germany.

Germany has prospered in recent decades. Frankfurt is a worldwide financial center.

Under the Basic Law

G ERMANY IS A DEMOCRACY OFFICIALLY CALLED the Federal Republic of Germany. *Federal* means that the government gets its power from the divisions or states that form it. Germany is made up of sixteen different states, called *Länder* (the singular is *Land*). Germany is governed by its constitution, called the Basic Law, which was approved in 1949. The people of East Germany voted to approve the Basic Law when they became part of the Federal Republic of Germany in 1990.

Opposite: **The Reichstag was built to house the parliament of the German Empire. It was damaged in a fire in 1933 and was not fully reconstructed until after reunification.**

Running the Government

Germany's legislature consists of a two-house parliament. The lower house, called the Bundestag, has at least 598 representatives. German citizens elect them to four-year terms. The Bundestag meets in Berlin in a historic domed building called the Reichstag.

The upper house is called the Bundesrat. Its members are appointed by the governments of the sixteen states and vary in number depending on population of the states. Bundesrat members are appointed to five-year terms, but the states can replace

The German flag is made up of three horizontal stripes of black, dark red, and yellow. German nationalists who opposed Napoléon's rule used this same flag in 1813. It was then chosen as the flag of the Weimar Republic in 1919 but was dropped under the Nazi regime. In 1949, the Federal Republic of Germany adopted it as the nation's official flag.

them before their terms are up. The Bundesrat meets in Berlin in a building that was originally the Prussian House of Lords.

When citizens vote for the Bundestag, they cast two votes. The first chooses their specific representative. The second is cast for people suggested by specific political parties. The second vote gives parties additional strength in the Bundestag.

People casting ballots in Berlin. Germans must be at least eighteen years old to vote.

Chancellor Angela Merkel

Angela Merkel achieved several "firsts" when she became the German chancellor in 2005. She was the first woman to become chancellor and the first chancellor of the Federal Republic of Germany who was raised in East Germany. She is also the first chancellor born after World War II.

She was born Angela Kasner in Hamburg, West Germany, in 1954. Her father was a Lutheran minister who moved to East Germany, hoping to help keep the church alive there. She studied chemistry at college and earned a PhD in chemistry from the University of Leipzig. She was working as a chemist when the Berlin Wall was torn down.

Merkel immediately became involved in the growing democracy movement in East Germany. She joined the Christian Democratic Union, a conservative party, and was elected to the first parliament of a reunified Germany. In 1991, Chancellor Helmut Kohl appointed her to his cabinet, as minister for women and youth. She quickly rose through the government. In 2000, she was elected the leader of her party, and five years later, she became chancellor.

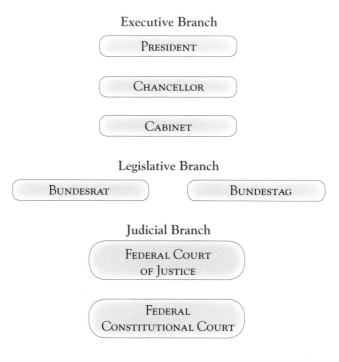

NATIONAL GOVERNMENT OF GERMANY

Executive Branch

PRESIDENT

CHANCELLOR

CABINET

Legislative Branch

BUNDESRAT   BUNDESTAG

Judicial Branch

FEDERAL COURT
OF JUSTICE

FEDERAL
CONSTITUTIONAL COURT

The members of the Bundestag elect the head of the government, called the chancellor. He or she is typically the candidate of the party that holds the most seats in the Bundestag.

There are no limits on how many terms the chancellor may serve. The chancellor chooses the cabinet members, who oversee different activities and concerns of the government. For example, there is a minister of defense, a minister of finance, and a minister of education and research.

Germany also has a president, who is the head of state. This position is mainly ceremonial. The president is elected by members of the Bundestag and the state legislatures.

The National Anthem

In 1841, August Heinrich Hoffmann von Fallersleben wrote the words to "Deutschlandlied," or "Song of Germany," which was set to music by composer Joseph Haydn. In 1922, the first verse of this song became the national anthem of the new German republic. The verse begins, "*Deutschland, Deutschland über alles*," meaning "Germany, Germany above all." During the Nazi era, people the world over came to hate this line. In 1952, the third verse of the song became the national anthem of the Federal Republic of Germany, and it remains the anthem of the reunified Germany.

German lyrics

Einigkeit und Recht und Freiheit
Für das deutsche Vaterland!
Danach lasst uns alle streben
Brüderlich mit Herz und Hand!
Einigkeit und Recht und Freiheit
Sind des Glückes Unterpfand;
Blüh' im Glanze dieses Glückes,
Blühe, deutsches Vaterland!

English translation

Unity and law and freedom
For the German Fatherland
Let us all strive for that
In brotherhood with heart and hand!
Unity and law and freedom
Are the foundation for happiness
Bloom in the glow of happiness
Bloom, German Fatherland.

Germany has several different kinds of courts. Court cases are divided among different courts, depending on whether they have to do with law, taxes, labor disputes, or social cases. Criminal and most civil cases are tried in ordinary courts. Appellate courts review decisions made in local or regional ordinary courts. The highest ordinary court is the Federal Court of Justice.

Germany also has several specialized courts that deal with cases concerning tax law, labor law, and insurance issues.

The Federal Constitutional Court determines whether laws passed by the legislature follow the German constitution. This court includes sixteen judges, eight of whom are named by the Bundestag, and eight by the Bundesrat.

The judges on the Federal Constitutional Court are elected to twelve-year terms. They must retire at age sixty-eight.

The States

When the German Empire was created in 1871, it was made up of twenty-five states. Long ago, most of them had been separate nations. When West Germany was formed in 1949, some of those states were combined, so the new nation had eleven states. East Germany consisted of five states.

Today, these sixteen states make up the Federal Republic of Germany. Berlin, Hamburg, and Bremen are the three smallest states. They are city-states, meaning they are cities with a small amount of land around them. The other states spread across large areas.

States

The largest state by area is Bavaria, in the southeast. It is a bit smaller than the U.S. state of South Carolina. The largest by population is North Rhine-Westphalia, with eighteen million people. It includes Düsseldorf, its capital, and the big industrial area of the Ruhr Valley.

Each state has its own parliament, which makes decisions for that state. The national parliament makes decisions that affect the nation as a whole.

Military Service

Beginning in the mid-1950s, young German men were required to serve in the military. They usually did their military service

Angela Merkel speaks to José Manuel Barroso, the president of the European Commission, the executive branch of the European Union.

before going to university or getting a job. They could choose to do alternative service, such as helping out in communities if they preferred. This policy of required service ended in 2011, but the Basic Law allows it to be restarted if necessary.

Joining Nations

Other nations around the globe hope that Germany will become more involved in global politics, but many Germans are not interested. They have, however, tried to take the lead on environmental problems. A Green Party formed in Germany in 1979 to focus on the environment. It was one of the first such groups and became one of the best known.

The success of the Marshall Plan laid the groundwork for European nations to work together economically in what eventually became the European Union. Having twice been at the center of wars that were disastrous for the world, Germany now prefers to work together with other countries.

A Look at the Capital

Berlin's history dates back almost a thousand years. During that time it was the capital of Prussia, and later of various German states through Hitler's Third Reich. When Germany was divided after World War II, Berlin was also divided. The part of Berlin controlled by the Soviet Union became East Berlin, the capital of East Germany. West Germany's capital moved to the city of Bonn, near Cologne. Since reunification, Berlin is once again the capital of Germany. Today the city is home to about 3.4 million people.

A mixture of old and new, Berlin features palaces, cathedrals, museums, concert halls, and universities. The city has grand boulevards, such as Ku'damm (short for Kurfürstendamm) and Unter den Linden (meaning "under the linden trees"), and funky neighborhoods.

The tallest structure in Germany is the television tower, standing 1,207 feet (368 m) tall, in the eastern sector of the city.

The heart of the German government is the Reichstag, which was built to house the parliament of the German Empire. It was partially destroyed by fire in 1933 and was left in ruins for decades. After reunification, it was completely reconstructed and is once again the meeting place of the Bundestag. Nearby is the Brandenburg Gate (below), one of the city's best-known landmarks. After the Berlin Wall came down, it was the site of many celebrations.

Modes of transportation in the city range from buses and trams and subways to ferries that travel on the many rivers and canals that cut through the city.

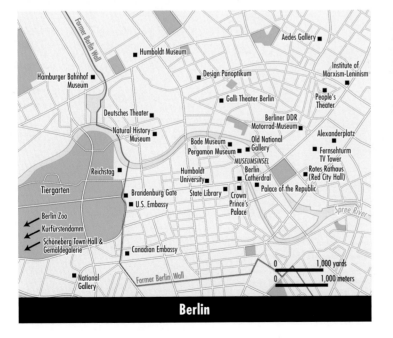

Berlin

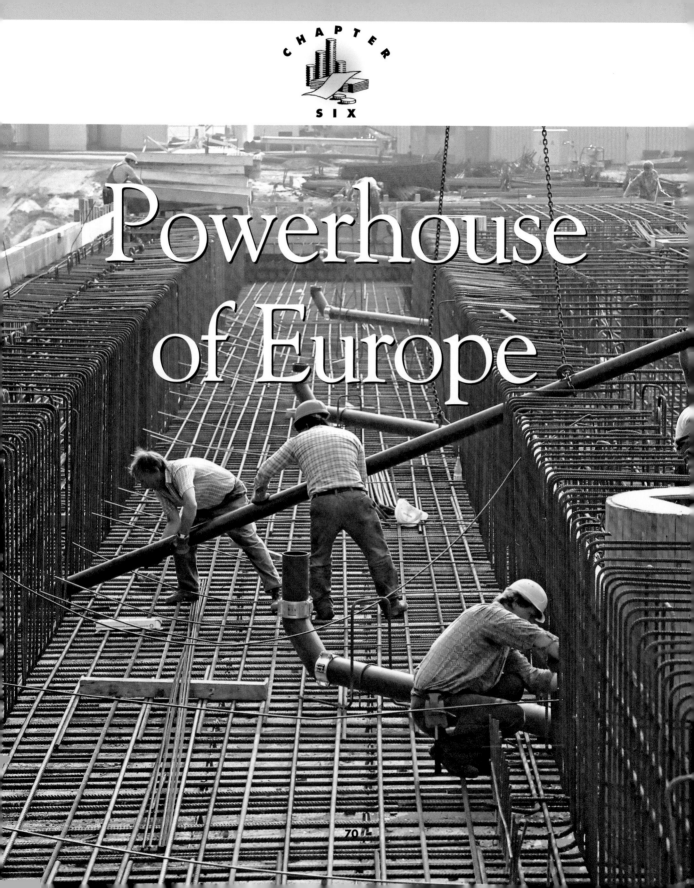

CHAPTER SIX

Powerhouse of Europe

IMMEDIATELY AFTER WORLD WAR II, MANY PEOPLE IN Germany were hungry and homeless. Cities were devastated. In 1948, the United States began putting huge amounts of money into rebuilding the European countries destroyed by the war. This was called the Marshall Plan, after U.S. secretary of state George Marshall. By the end of four years, every nation that received funds was doing better economically than it had been before the war.

Opposite: **Construction workers ease a pipe into place. More than 2.5 million people in Germany work in the construction industry.**

The Economic Miracle

West Germany and several other nations formed the European Economic Community in 1957 to help each other economically. Over time, this organization became the European Union (EU), which today has twenty-seven member countries. Many of Germany's economic decisions have been turned over to the EU.

The Soviet Union, which controlled East Germany, did not join the EU nor did it put money into improving conditions in

Boys play on an old car next to a crumbling wall in East Germany in the 1970s. While Germany was divided, East Germany suffered and West Germany prospered.

East Germany. By the time Germany was reunited, East Germany was in bad shape. The roads were crumbling, factories had deteriorated, and the cities were desolate. After reunification, the new nation passed the Solidarity Pact. Federal, state, and local governments were required to help rebuild the eastern sector. New roads, shopping malls, and houses were built. Although the situation in eastern Germany has improved significantly, the economy there still lags behind western Germany. In the east, incomes are lower and unemployment is higher.

But as a whole, Germany is thriving. It has the fourth-largest economy in the world and is one of the world's leading exporters.

Agriculture

Four-fifths of German land is fairly flat and fertile, making it good for agriculture and forestry. Wheat, corn, potatoes, and sugar beets grow well in the plains of the north. A vivid yellow plant called yellow rapeseed or field mustard also grows in this region. A relative of the cabbage, rapeseed is used to produce canola oil and is fed to cattle.

Cattle and pigs are raised on rougher land, such as the foothills and mountain slopes. In the river valleys, grapes

Germany is one of the top producers of rapeseed in the European Union.

are grown to make wine. Bavaria also grows barley and hops, which are used in making beer.

Made in Germany

A huge variety of goods commonly sold in North America are manufactured in Germany. They include Volkswagen cars, Bayer aspirin, Adidas and Puma athletic shoes, Leica cameras, Zeiss lenses, Nivea face cream, Melitta coffee filters, and Haribo gummy bears. Germany's major exports are machine and electrical parts, medicines, and other chemicals.

What Germany Grows, Makes, and Mines

Agriculture (2009)

Wheat	25,190,300 metric tons
Milk	27,938,000 metric tons
Sugar beets	25,919,000 metric tons

Manufacturing (2005, value added by manufacturing)

Motor vehicles	US$56,071,000,000
Machinery	US$45,036,000,000
Metal products	US$39,114,000,000

Mining (2009)

Salt	18,393,000 metric tons
Kaolin	4,514,000 metric tons
Potash	1,825,000 metric tons

Germany had been known for its heavy industry since the early 1800s, when factories in the Ruhr Valley, where great supplies of coal were available, began producing steel. This steel industry allowed Germans to build the tanks and other equipment it needed for war. Today, Germany produces more products made out of steel than steel itself. It buys the additional steel it needs from China.

ThyssenKrupp AG is one of the world's largest manufacturers. It makes heavy equipment such as trains and elevators and employs hundreds of thousands of people around the world. Siemens, which is even larger, makes thousands of products related to energy and health. Wind turbines, water filtration plants, and medical equipment are among its products.

Resources

		C	Coal
Grains	Dairy, livestock	Fe	Iron ore
Cereals	Fruit	A	Oil
		K	Potash
Mixed	Forests	U	Uranium
		Zn	Zinc

The Scent of Cologne

The scented liquid called cologne, which has a lighter scent than perfume, is named after the German city of Cologne. One of the earliest and most popular colognes was invented for men in Cologne in the early 1700s by the Italian perfume maker Giovanni Maria Farina. At first it was called Eau de Cologne ("water of Cologne"), but was later renamed 4711 after the address of the building where Farina worked.

As early as the 1870s, Karl Benz and other people were designing automobiles in Germany. Soon, the Mercedes-Benz and the BMW were being produced for a world market. In the 1930s, Adolf Hitler ordered that a "people's car" (*Volkswagen*) be built. All of those cars are still produced.

Some of the world's earliest motorways for high-speed automobiles were built in Germany in the 1930s. Today,

Germany produces more cars than any other nation in Europe. Its major manufacturers include Audi, BMW, Mercedes-Benz, and Volkswagen.

Germany's freeway system is called the Autobahn. In most places, it has no speed limit for cars.

There are many other ways to get around Germany quickly. It is part of a European-wide railway system. High-speed trains link the major cities. Frankfurt is the site of one of the world's busiest airports. It serves more than fifty million passengers every year. Munich, Düsseldorf, and Berlin also have major airports.

Energy for the Future

Although Germany has huge coal supplies, it is working on developing forms of energy that do not harm the environment as coal does. The nation is committed to significantly reducing harmful pollutants. To achieve that, the German government requires that all new buildings be energy efficient, and that older buildings be improved if possible.

The German-Russian Pipeline

In 2011, Germany and Russia built a pipeline to carry natural gas from Russia to the European Union. Called the Nord Stream Pipeline, it runs under the Baltic Sea. It is the longest sub-sea pipeline in the world, stretching across 759 miles (1,222 km). In Germany, the pipeline ends at Greifswald. From there, natural gas is distributed to EU countries. Building the pipeline was controversial because some people were concerned that it could cause environmental damage. Others did not want the EU to have to rely on Russia for its energy. The natural gas supply is expected to be delivered through this pipeline for at least fifty years.

Already, more than one-fifth of the nation's energy comes from renewable sources, such as wind power. Much solar

Germany gets more than 10 percent of its energy from wind power.

power, energy from the sun, is generated in Erlasee Solar Park in Bavaria, one of the sunniest parts of Germany. The solar panels move with the sun. For many years this site produced more solar power than any other location in the world.

Communications

Bertelsmann, one of the largest media companies in the world, started as a publisher in 1835. It now owns Random House, the largest publisher in the United States, as well as other companies around the world. Their headquarters are in Gütersloh. The largest book fair in the world is held each year in Frankfurt. Publishers from all over the world come to meet other publishers who could translate and sell their books.

Gutenberg and His Printing Press

Johannes Gutenberg introduced a new way of printing books to Europe in the mid-fifteenth century, with the invention of movable type. This started a printing revolution. Gutenberg printed the Bible around 1456 using metal type carved with individual letters, so that the letters could be rearranged to make new words. The letters could be used over and over again. Prior to Gutenberg's invention, whole words, even whole pages of text, had been carved out of wood and used for printing. Books were very expensive, and only the wealthy could afford them. With reusable letters, books could be printed much more cheaply than before, so less wealthy people could afford them as well.

Nearly three hundred thousand people attend the Frankfurt Book Fair each year.

The largest national newspaper is the *Bild*, which means "picture." Most German newspapers are regional rather than national. Many cities support at least two daily newspapers. Germans also make heavy use of the Internet.

The Currency and Its Crisis

The euro was introduced in 2002 as the currency for twelve of the nations in the European Union. Today, seventeen EU countries have replaced their old currencies with the euro. These countries are known as the Eurozone.

After the euro was introduced, the European Union thrived for a time, but then the economy began to stumble. Starting in 2008, jobs disappeared, people and governments owed more money than they could repay, and the euro became very unstable. Unemployment skyrocketed in some countries. It rose to 24 percent in Spain, 22 percent in Greece, and 10.2 percent in France and Italy in 2012. Germany had the healthiest economy in the EU. In 2012, its unemployment rate was only 5.4 percent.

Germany had never let its economy get out of control. It had developed its economy, invested in technology, and increased exports. Thus, it had become the wealthiest and most powerful country in the Eurozone.

Visitors relax near the town hall in Munich. Tourism is an important part of the German economy. Millions of foreign tourists visit the country every year, enjoying its charming cities and peaceful countryside.

Angela Merkel was reelected as chancellor in 2009, promising Germans that the problems of other EU nations would not produce major reforms that might harm Germany. She insisted that the other countries begin austerity programs in order to receive help from the Eurozone banking system. Under austerity, the countries must carry out programs such as raising taxes, cutting government spending, and reducing payments to the elderly. Austerity proved impossible in some countries. Too many people were out of work and had nothing to live on. Greece, in particular, threatened to pull out of the Eurozone. This would harm all Eurozone countries.

Merkel at first held firm in favor of austerity. The alternative was for the EU to invest money in growing the economies

Money Facts

Germany's currency is the euro, a currency used in seventeen countries across Europe. The symbol for the euro is €. One euro is divided into one hundred cents. Euro coins come in values of 1, 2, 5, 10, 20, and 50 cents, and 1 and 2 euros. Each country issues its own coins. The country designs the front of the coins themselves, while the backs of the coins show a map of Europe. Some German coins show an oak twig, others show the Brandenburg Gate in Berlin, and still others show an eagle. Euro bills, or banknotes, come in values of 5, 10, 20, 50, 100, 200, and 500 euros. The front of each bill has an image or gateway and the back features a bridge. Each denomination is a different color. In 2012, €1.00 equaled US$1.25, and US$1.00 equaled €0.80.

of the troubled countries. Merkel gradually accepted that the combination of austerity and growth would be better. But she insisted that if Germany were to pay into a system to help other countries recover, those countries would have to agree to tighter controls on spending.

The problems in the Eurozone have not been solved, and they won't be fixed easily. Whatever happens, Germany will play an increasingly important role in the economy of Europe, and the world, in the years to come.

German chancellor Angela Merkel and French president François Hollande lead the two wealthiest countries in the Eurozone.

Speaking of Germans

84

THE OFFICIAL LANGUAGE OF GERMANY IS GERMAN, but there are many dialects, or versions, of German. The way it is spoken depends on what part of the country a person lives in. All told, over 95 percent of the people speak German. It is the most widely spoken language in the European Union after English.

Unlike English, nouns in German can be feminine, masculine, or neutral. Feminine nouns use *die* for "the," masculine use *der*, and neutral use *das*. Some examples are *das Jahr* (the year), *die Sonne* (the sun), and *der Garten* (the garden). In German, all nouns are capitalized. And German often combines adjectives to a noun to make one long word. For example, "maximum speed limit" is *Hoechsgeschwindigkeitsbegrenzung.*

New German

In 1996, the German-speaking countries of Germany, Austria, Lichtenstein, and Switzerland agreed that it was time to simplify German spellings. People objected to some of the changes, and they were eventually dropped. One change that

Opposite: **About 13 percent of Germans are under age fifteen. The nation's population is shrinking as people have fewer children.**

Even though some letters in the German alphabet, like ß, are no longer used, older street signs still include them.

has remained was eliminating a letter in the German alphabet called the Eszett (ß). Words that once had the ß are now written with an *ss* instead, so *daß* ("that") is now spelled *dass*.

Like all languages, the German language changes as the world changes. A dictionary called *Duden* shows the spelling of German words. Today, *Duden* is adding many technological terms. Recently added were *skypen*, meaning "to use Skype," and *twittern*, "to Twitter."

Common German Terms

ja	yes
nein	no
bitte	please; you're welcome
danke	thank you
guten Tag	good day; hello
auf Wiedersehen	good-bye
Wie geht es ihnen?	How are you?
Ich verstehe nicht.	I don't understand.

The Umlaut

Many German words have two dots over an *a*, *o*, or *u*. Those dots are called an umlaut. It changes the sound of the vowel, giving it a bit of a twist so that it sounds a bit like there is an *e* after it. Many people in the United States originally came from Germany with the name Müller. When the umlaut was dropped, some people turned the name into Muller, some into Miller, and some stuck with the umlaut sound and made it Mueller.

Other Languages

Some Germans speak other languages, which are officially recognized. They live in areas that were once parts of other countries.

About fifty thousand people of Danish descent live in northern Germany near the border with Denmark. These people were cut off from Denmark in 1920 when a vote by

The Frisian Islands are a popular vacation spot.

the people divided this area, called Schleswig, in half. Danes in Southern Schleswig often speak Danish, though they also speak German. Even after almost a century as German citizens, most still attend Danish schools.

In that same region, Frisian is spoken by about half a million people, primarily in the Frisian Islands in the North Sea. Germany recognizes Frisian as an official language. It is similar to English, but English people and the Frisians can't understand each other.

Near Poland, in the eastern states of Brandenburg and Saxony, live some Slavic people called Sorbs or Wends. Their territory, which includes an extension into Poland, is called Lusatia, and their language is Lusatian. There are about one hundred thousand Sorbs in Germany. Sorbs are recognized as an official minority, and, like the Danes of Schleswig, have their own schools.

In recent years, many Romani have moved into Germany from Romania and Bulgaria.

The wars of the 1700s and 1800s destroyed the economies of many small German states. Rather than remain in their homelands with no prospects of improving their lives, many people chose to immigrate to the British colonies of North America. Within a few short years, more than a million Germans had moved to the colonies, especially New York and Pennsylvania. One immigrant, John Jacob Astor (left), became the wealthiest man in America. Eventually more than eight million Germans moved to America, and today about fifty million Americans claim German ancestry, which is more than claim any other ethnic group.

About seventy thousand Romani, or Roma, people live in Germany. They speak a language related to Hindi, which is spoken in India. Romani people were among those who were killed by the Nazi regime.

The Ausländer

By the mid-1950s, West Germany was booming, and there were not enough people to do all the work that needed to be done. At the same time, the nation of Turkey, on the southeastern border of Europe, did not have enough work for its growing population. To help both these problems, West Germany created a "guest-worker" program. Thousands of Turks soon moved to West Germany.

The guest-worker program lasted until 1973, when the German economy took a downturn. Some Turks went home,

Children of German citizens are automatically German citizens themselves, regardless of where they were born.

Ethnic Groups in Germany (2010)

German	91.5%
Turkish	2.4%
Other (including Greek, Italian, Polish, Russian, Serbian, Spanish)	6.1%

but others had brought their families to Germany and settled down there, so they stayed. There were still not enough jobs in Turkey during this time.

Today, about fifteen million people in Germany are of non-German descent. That is the highest percentage of immigrants of any nation in the European Union. Only Russia and the United States have a greater percentage of immigrants. In Germany, immigrants and their children are known as the *Ausländer*, the "foreigners."

Unlike in the United States, a baby born in Germany is not automatically a German citizen. A child born in Germany is a citizen if at least one parent is a German citizen. However, if neither parent is a German citizen, the child can only be a citizen from birth if at that time one of the parents has lived in Germany legally for eight years and has a permanent residence permit. When grown, that child must reapply to become a citizen on his or her own.

Many Turks have never acquired German citizenship. Most Turkish residents are Muslims, followers of the religion Islam, and remain apart from the rest of German society. Even if their family has been in Germany for half a century, they are often still viewed as foreigners. A professor in Berlin who was born in Turkey said in 2011, "I'm a German citizen. I have a German child. I'm devoting my career to educating the young people who will run the country in the next generation. But I'm still seen as a foreigner."

Turkish women dance at a festival in Berlin. Turks are the largest minority group in Germany.

Integrating Immigrants

Throughout most of its recent history, Germany has insisted that only people of German heritage could be citizens. Chancellor Angela Merkel, however, realized that Germany needed to more fully integrate the immigrants and children of immigrants into the nation. Studies show that many young Turkish people in Germany are not succeeding in school. In 2009, only 9 percent of the Turkish students passed the test that would allow them to go to university.

People shop in a neighborhood in Berlin called Little Istanbul. Some Turkish people remain separate from the larger German society.

Germany has spent a huge amount of money to provide services for immigrants, especially to teach them German, hoping this would strengthen their ability to be fully a part of German society. This was part of a program to attract skilled workers, especially in the technology fields. But so far the effort has not been successful. Skilled workers have not been moving to Germany, and people who come to attend university go home afterward. There are thousands of engineering and other skilled-worker jobs available with no one to fill them.

Some cities are trying to attract skilled workers in other ways. The city of Düsseldorf has invited Japanese and Chinese companies to establish themselves there. About seventy-five thousand Chinese now live in Germany.

Chinese students in Berlin attend a celebration of the anniversary of the German constitution.

Many Germans live in small cities.

Germany's Largest Cities (2011 est.)

Berlin	3,439,100
Hamburg	1,769,117
Munich	1,220,440
Cologne	998,105
Frankfurt	695,000

Where People Live

Germany has a population of about eighty-two million. Most people live in medium-size cities. The only truly large cities in Germany are Berlin, Hamburg, Munich, and Cologne, each of which has a population of close to or more than a million. There are at least eighty German cities that have populations between one hundred thousand and one million.

Young and Old

Most couples in Germany have one or two children. In fact, Germans are having so few children that the population is shrinking. Germany has tried to encourage parents to have larger families by giving them what is called "parents' money," so they can take more time off work to care for their children. But this program has not been successful. In most German families, both parents work, and daycare is often not available.

In Germany, people on average live to age eighty, and the number of elderly is increasing. The government provides the elderly with many benefits. Some people are concerned that as the national population shrinks, the working population will have a hard time supporting the large numbers of elderly people.

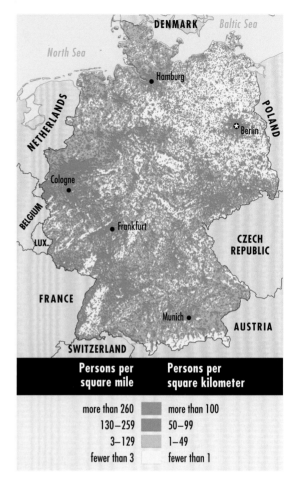

Persons per square mile	Persons per square kilometer
more than 260	more than 100
130–259	50–99
3–129	1–49
fewer than 3	fewer than 1

Twenty-one percent of Germans are age sixty-five or older.

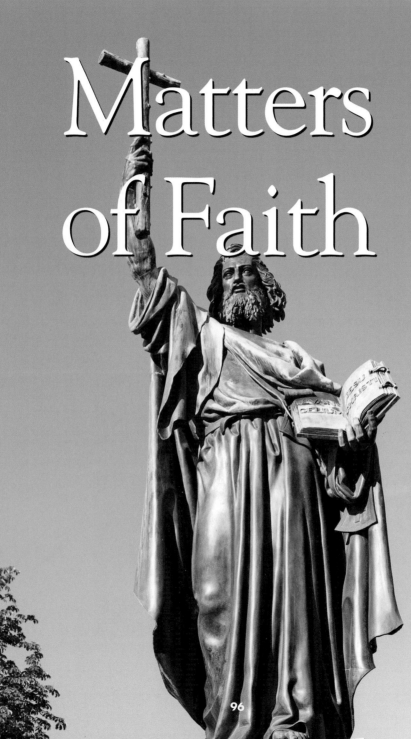

Matters of Faith

96

LONG AGO, THE NATIVE GERMAN TRIBES WORSHIPPED the god Wotan, a figure in Norse mythology. They began to come in contact with Christianity when they brought prisoners back from the Balkan region, in southeastern Europe, which had already become Christian. Wulfila, the son of one of these prisoners, translated the Bible into Gothic, the language of the Goths, in about 350 CE. He had to invent an alphabet in order to write this translation.

St. Boniface, an English monk, was an important figure in bringing Christianity to Germany. In the eighth century, he arrived in the region to try to convince the Frankish people to become Christian. St. Boniface and fifty-two other Christians were murdered by the Frisians who did not want their land to become Christian. St. Boniface is now the patron saint of Germany.

Opposite: **St. Boniface spread Christianity in what is now Germany. He is buried in Fulda Cathedral in central Germany.**

Martin Luther challenged the authority and teachings of the Roman Catholic Church.

Religion in Germany

Protestant	34%
Roman Catholic	34%
Muslim	4%
Other or Unaffiliated	28%

Protestant and Catholic

The Protestant Reformation began in Germany when Martin Luther nailed to the door of Wittenberg Cathedral a list of his objections to the behavior of the Roman Catholic Church. Today, Germany is home to roughly an equal number of Protestants and Catholics. Most Protestants live in the north. They are mostly Lutherans, though other denominations such as Methodist, Baptist, and Mormon are also represented in Germany. Bavaria, in the south, is the center of Catholic Germany.

The small town of Oberammergau in Bavaria is known for its Passion play, a theatrical story of the last week in the life of

Reaching Toward Heaven

Cologne Cathedral (left) is one of the most spectacular examples of Gothic architecture in the world. Gothic architecture began during the twelfth century. It is marked by soaring ceilings and pointed arches. When Cologne Cathedral was built, its towers were the tallest in the world, reaching heights of 515 feet (157 m). Though construction of the cathedral started in the thirteenth century, the structure stood incomplete for six hundred years. The towers were finally completed in 1880. During World War II, when many German cities were destroyed, Cologne Cathedral endured many bombings but remained standing and was eventually restored. *Münster*

Today, Ulm Minster, a Lutheran church in the city of Ulm, in southern Germany, is the tallest church in the world. It soars 530 feet (162 m) high. Like Cologne Cathedral, its construction was begun centuries ago. It began as a Catholic church, but by the time it was completed in 1890 it had become a Protestant church. It also survived World War II, while the city around it lay in ruins.

Jesus, whom Christians believe is the son of God. In 1634, a terrible plague killed large numbers of people across Europe. The people of Oberammergau promised God that they would put on a glorious production of a Passion play every ten years if they were spared. No villagers died, and the people of Oberammergau kept their promise. Travelers come from all over the world to watch the performance, which is put on by most of the people of the town. The stage can hold eight hundred actors.

Religion in the Nazi Era

When Adolf Hitler and the Nazi Party took control of Germany in 1933, they made an agreement with the Vatican, the headquarters of the Roman Catholic Church. The church agreed to stay out of politics, and the party agreed to let the church continue to educate children in Catholic schools. But the agreement did not hold. The Nazi government soon abolished all Catholic schools. Leaders in the Lutheran church formed a group opposed to the Nazis, under the leadership of Dietrich Bonhoeffer (right) and Martin Niemöller. Some of these leaders, including Bonhoeffer, were executed.

The Church in East Germany

Almost one-third of the people in Germany say they have no religious affiliation. Most of them live in the areas that were once East Germany. This is because the Communist government there had tried to destroy interest in religion.

Chancellor Angela Merkel's father was a minister who moved to East Germany to be near his hometown of Berlin. He tried to make the Communist viewpoint work within the church. The Soviet-controlled government decided to let the churches continue to function. They thought that soon only older people would care, and religion would wither away. That did not happen, but church membership dropped from 90 percent to 30 percent. After reunification, few former East Germans returned to religion.

The Shrinking Church

Most Germans say they believe in God, but the number who go to church has shrunk in recent decades. It is estimated that only 10 percent of German Christians go to church on Sundays, and most of them are elderly.

Most churches don't depend on contributions from the churchgoers to survive. People who pay taxes are supporting the churches and paying the salaries of the ministers and priests. When people move to a new city or town, they must register with that town. When they register, they choose whether their taxes will support Catholic churches, Protestant churches, Jewish synagogues, or Muslim mosques. Beginning in the 1980s, many people began objecting to the taxes. Many people have withdrawn from supporting both Catholic and Protestant churches.

The percentage of people who attend church services in Germany has been dropping since the end of World War II.

The German Pope

Since 2005, the head of the Roman Catholic Church has been Benedict XVI, who was born Joseph Ratzinger. A native of Marktl in Bavaria, he was a professor of religion before becoming an important figure at the Vatican, the headquarters of the church in Rome, Italy. Benedict XVI is the first pope in almost a thousand years to have been born in what is now Germany.

Some churches do not take tax money. They are called free churches and depend on their members to support them.

Muslims

Islam is the second-largest religion in Germany after Christianity. In 2009, about 4.3 million Muslims lived in Germany. Less than half of them are German citizens. Most live in Berlin and other large cities. There are mosques, Muslim houses of worship, in most cities. The nation's oldest active mosque is in Berlin. It was built in the 1920s.

About three-quarters of Germany's Muslims belong to the Sunni sect of Islam. It is the dominant form of Islam in Turkey. A much smaller Muslim sect in Germany is the Alevis. They worship through music and dance. In this sect, unlike most Muslim groups, men and women worship together.

Jews and Buddhists

An estimated 250,000 Buddhists live in Germany. Probably half are immigrants from Asia.

Before World War II, Germany was home to at least a half million Jews. In the months after Adolf Hitler came to power in the 1930s, thousands of Jews left Germany, never to return. Most of the rest who stayed were killed. By 1950, only thirty-seven thousand Jews remained in Germany.

The number of Jews in Germany is increasing, as many have emigrated from Russia in recent years. Today, about one hundred thousand Jewish people live in Germany. Berlin and Munich have the largest Jewish populations in Germany.

People attend a ceremony marking the opening of a synagogue in Schwerin, in northern Germany. The new synagogue is built on the site of a synagogue that was destroyed during the Nazi era.

Music, Arts, and Sports

T HE ARTS HAVE BEEN IMPORTANT TO GERMANS ever since the early Germanic tribes began to make drawings on stone. Their pictures told tales of the wondrous actions of the gods. Then, as writing developed, they recorded their thoughts on every subject. Today, much of Europe's culture stems from Germany.

Classical Music

Germans are at the top of the list of the greatest classical music composers. Johann Sebastian Bach (1685–1750) spent many years writing new music both as a court musician and a church organist. His work remains popular today with pianists, organists, and singers. Ludwig van Beethoven (1770–1827) began to go deaf around age twenty-six. At the time, he had written only two long musical compositions called symphonies. He wrote seven more after becoming deaf, when he could hear the music only in his head. Johannes Brahms (1833–1897) composed

great piano, symphony, and choral pieces. George Frideric Handel (1685–1759) was born in Germany but was living in England when he wrote *Messiah*, the best known and most frequently performed choral work in all of classical music.

Richard Wagner (1813–1883) wrote operas that are still staged today. Wagner had a theater built just for his operas in the town of Bayreuth, near the Czech border. His music is celebrated each year at the Bayreuth Festival, one of the world's great music festivals. The performances are so popular that people sometimes have to wait ten years to get tickets.

In addition to being a composer, Ludwig van Beethoven was also an accomplished pianist. He had to give up performing when he lost his hearing.

Popular Music

Popular music in Germany includes a wide variety of styles. They range from oompah bands that play folk music for tourists to all kinds of rock music. Today, Germany is the fourth-largest music market in the world.

Probably the best-selling German group was the Scorpions, a heavy metal group that started in Hanover in the 1960s. Germany is the center of electronic music called techno.

A group called Kraftwerk ("power station") popularized electronic music with its driving rhythms. In East Berlin, techno had to be performed in secret before the Berlin Wall fell, but the music brought young people together after reunification. Germany also gave birth to trance music. It, too, is primarily electronic and has driving rhythms, but it uses traditional instruments. Trance music is more melodic than techno.

In the 1970s, the band Kraftwerk popularized electronic music. Kraftwerk still performs today.

Berlin and Munich are the homes of German hip-hop. Musicians in Munich have begun German-Turkish hip-hop. Sung in both German and Turkish, the songs about the immigrant experience have spread to Turkey itself.

Art and Artists

Until recent times, most German art was religious. Fifteenth-century painter and printmaker Albrecht Dürer (1471–1528) created amazing altarpieces for churches, but he is equally well known for a simple picture of a rabbit. Dürer used his skill at making engravings and woodcuts to make prints of pictures. Another German painter, Hans Holbein the Elder (ca. 1465–1524), painted many religious images. His son Hans Holbein the Younger (ca. 1497–1543) was one of the greatest portraitists of the sixteenth century.

Albrecht Dürer painted this self-portrait in 1498.

All major German cities have great museums. Berlin's Museumsinsel, meaning "museum island," has a collection of museums. The first one opened in 1830 when Prussian king Friedrich Wilhelm III decided that all royal art should be available to the public. Other buildings in the Museumsinsel house ancient antiques, portraits, contemporary art, and one of the great collections of world coins.

Hildegard of Bingen was both a composer and a writer. Her writings contained discussions of herbal medicine and descriptions of the natural world, including plants, animals, and rocks.

Literature

Germany's earliest literature was written in Latin, the language of the Roman Catholic Church. Hildegard of Bingen (1098–1179) wrote dramas, poems, and medical books. She also composed music and is probably the first composer to be identified. Another poet of the time was Ava, the first woman known to have written in a European language.

Literature has remained important throughout German history. Johann Wolfgang von Goethe of Frankfurt was a poet who is best remembered for his tale of a scholar named Faust. Faust sells his soul to Mephistopheles, the Devil, in return for complete knowledge. In the end, Faust is not turned evil by the Devil, because his search for knowledge is a good thing.

Fairy Tale Road

For 370 miles (595 km), travelers can explore Germany's history of fairy tales. The journey starts in Hanau, Hessen, where the Grimm brothers, Jacob and Wilhelm, lived in the 1800s and collected folk tales. The brothers traveled through the region talking to people. They wrote up the tales they heard. Today, museums and statues recall the tales of Little Red Riding Hood, Snow White, the Goose Girl, the Bremen Town Musicians, Rapunzel, the Pied Piper, Tom Thumb, Rumpelstiltskin, and many others.

The Nobel Prize in Literature has been awarded to writers of German literature many times. The first to win the honor was Theodor Mommsen in 1902, who wrote *The History of Rome*. Thomas Mann, author of *The Magic Mountain* and *Buddenbrooks*, won in 1929. Hermann Hesse, the winner in 1946, wrote *Siddhartha*, a novel about the Buddha, who began the Buddhist religion. The 1966 winner, Nelly Sachs, wrote plays and poetry about life under the Nazi regime. Günter Grass, the 1999 Nobel Prize winner, is often regarded as German, but he was born in Danzig, which now is part of Poland. His novels, especially *The Tin Drum*, deliver a powerful antiwar message.

Science and Invention

Since the Nobel Prizes were started in 1901, Germans or German-born people have won more than one hundred Nobel Prizes. Only the United States and the United Kingdom have won more. Wilhelm Conrad Roentgen won the very first prize in physics, given in 1901, for his discovery of roentgen rays, better known as X-rays. Emil Adolf von Behring also won that year for his discovery of a treatment for diphtheria and tetanus, diseases that killed hundreds of thousands of people every year.

Hermann Hesse wrote novels about people's search for spirituality.

The Father of Modern Physics

Albert Einstein, who was born in Ulm in 1879, is known as the father of modern physics. He created what has become the world's best-known equation, $E=mc^2$, which shows the relationship between mass and energy. He developed the theory of general relativity, an important idea that deals with space, time, and gravity. Einstein was awarded the Nobel Prize in Physics in 1921.

Einstein left Germany in 1932, shortly before the Nazis came to power in 1933. Since the Nazis were blaming Jews for Germany's problems, and Einstein was Jewish, he knew he would be in danger in his home country, so he never returned to Germany. He became a citizen of the United States in 1940 and lived the remainder of his life in Princeton, New Jersey.

Many important inventions and discoveries bear the names of Germans who developed them. These include the Geiger counter, the zeppelin airship, the diesel engine, the

Hans Geiger (left) and British scientist Ernest Rutherford with a Geiger counter, a machine they invented to detect radiation.

Bunsen burner, Fahrenheit temperature, Alzheimer's disease, Planck's
constant, and the Doppler effect.

Much of what has been learned
about the structure of the atom and
nuclear energy came from German
scientists such as Hans Bethe, Otto
Hahn, and Lise Meitner.

In 1912, German scientist Alfred
Wegener proposed the idea that all
of the continents were once part of a
giant landmass. When Wegener first
proposed this idea, people around the
world were skeptical. In the 1950s,
however, scientists began finding
evidence that his theory, called conti-
nental drift, was right. Wegener's ideas
began a revolution in scientists' under-
standing of the planet. Scientists now
know that the earth's outer layer is
broken into giant pieces that are slowly moving. This movement
is what formed the continents long ago, and it is what causes
earthquakes and volcanic eruptions today.

In addition to studying geol-
ogy and climate, Alfred
Wegener was also a polar
researcher. He made several
expeditions to Greenland to
study the glaciers there.

Soccer

About one-third of all Germans belong to sports clubs, where
they can play soccer. Children play wherever there is room,
and clubs compete on fields across the land.

Soccer is the most popular sport in Germany.

The World Cup tournament was first held in 1930. Except during World War II, it has been held every four years to determine the world's best soccer team. Germany has won the World Cup three times. Only Brazil and Italy have won more times.

The Women's World Cup has been played only six times. Germany's team has won twice, in 2003 and 2007. Birgit Prinz, a native of Frankfurt, is the only woman to play in three final tournaments. She was named the World Player of the Year three times. In 2011, the championship was held in Germany, with finals in Frankfurt. Japan took the title. It was the first time an Asian team won this competition.

Many world boxing championship matches have been held in Germany. Boxer Max Schmeling is remembered for having taken on and beaten the undefeated American Joe Louis in a 1936 bout. The two fought again in a 1938 rematch. Louis won this time, making him the first African American sports hero.

Motor racing is very popular in Germany, a country that produces such top cars as BMW, Mercedes, Audi, and Porsche. Anyone with a few dollars can drive on the historic racetrack called Nürburgring, south of Cologne. It is a public toll road,

The German soccer team celebrates winning the Women's World Cup in 2007.

but has a 13-mile (21 km) section where drivers can zoom along at race speeds. It has seventy-three curves, and many new cars are test-driven there.

German tennis players have won many tournaments around the world. Boris Becker and Steffi Graf are among the champions. Bernhard Langer was the first German golfer to win major international championships. He won the Masters in 1985 and 1993. More recently, Martin Kaymer has become one of the world's top golfers.

Boris Becker won forty-nine tennis singles titles during his career.

The Olympics

Germany participated in the first Olympic Games in 1896, and through the years Germans have been among the most successful athletes in the Games. German skiers, familiar with their home country's mountainous terrain, have always done well.

In 1936, both the Summer and the Winter Games were held in Germany. The Nazis wanted to make a big splash and hoped Germany would win most of the events. In the Summer Olympics, Germany did win the most medals, but African American track-and-field star Jesse Owens won eternal fame by winning four gold medals as Hitler looked on. In the Winter Olympics, Germany won the third most medals after Norway and Sweden.

The memory of the 1972 Summer Olympics, held in Munich, will always be marred by the murder of five Israeli athletes and six coaches. The Games were halted for twenty-four hours. The teams from some countries went home. Others stayed, but the life had gone out of the Olympics that year.

Jesse Owens (right) speeds ahead of the other runners at the 1936 Olympics. Owens won gold medals in the 100-meter race, the 200-meter race, the long jump, and the 4 x 100-meter relay race.

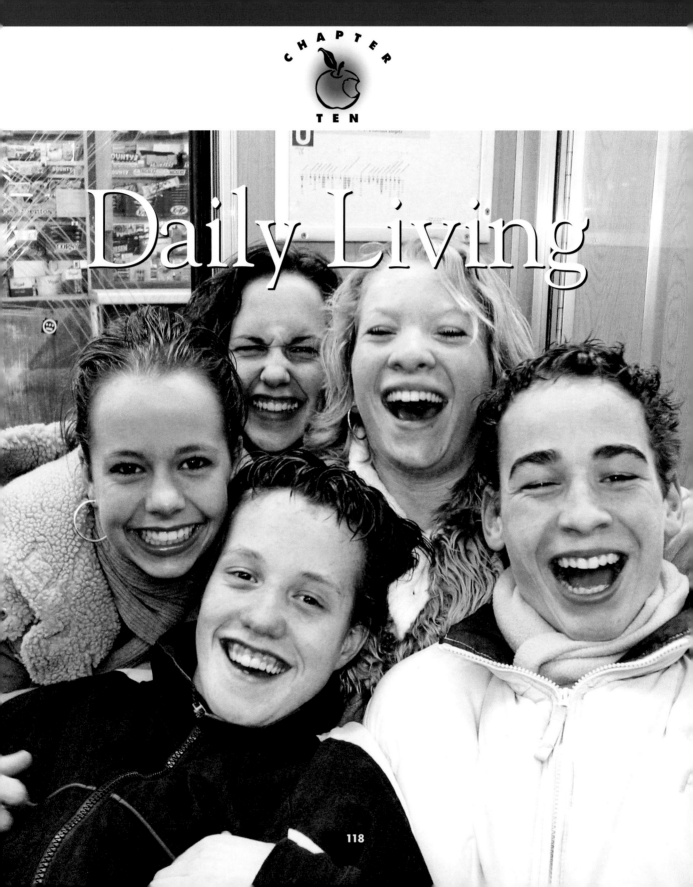

CHAPTER TEN

Daily Living

W
HEN OUTSIDERS THINK OF GERMANY, THEY
sometimes imagine men wearing leather pants called lederhosen, and women wearing colorful skirts called dirndls. These
are the traditional folk costumes from Bavaria. These types
of costumes are not everyday clothes. They are saved for
special events. In Germany, people dress the same as North
Americans do, whether they are at school, home, or work.

Education

By law, at three years old every child is guaranteed a chance
to go to kindergarten. But in fact, there are not enough kin-
dergartens for all the children.

Elementary school starts at age six and continues until age
ten or twelve. After that, students must choose among four different kinds of secondary education. The best students go to a
rigorous school called a *Gymnasium*, where they study intently
in preparation for college. Those who do not expect to go to
college will probably go to *Realschule*, which focuses on science

Kindergartens

Kindergarten was invented in Germany. Even its name is German. It means "children's garden." In 1837, educator Friedrich Froebel started a school that would help little children adjust from living at home all the time to going to school full time. Today, German children don't have to go to kindergarten. The choice is left to their parents.

and practical subjects and ends at grade 10. After that, students usually go on to vocational training or apprenticeships. Other students choose paths that combine the two kinds of education.

Most children in Germany go to public schools.

School runs from August to June or July. In most states, classes are held Monday through Friday, but in some places children go to school six days a week. Most of them, however, go to school only in the mornings.

Students at Gymnasium must pass a test called the *Abitur* to attend university. If they do not go to university, students must attend a vocational school or a part-time vocational school combined with part-time work until they are eighteen. Most universities are funded by the state in which they are located. More than half of the states charge no tuition.

The oldest university in Germany is Ruprecht-Karls-Universität, better known as Heidelberg University. It was founded in 1386. At least fifty-five of its students and faculty have received Nobel Prizes.

Heidelberg University is the most prestigious school in Germany.

Oktoberfest

Oktoberfest, in Munich, is one of the world's largest fairs. It takes place for sixteen days in September and October. Millions of visitors come to Munich at this time. The fair was first held in 1810 to celebrate the marriage of Crown

Prince Ludwig. That year, horse races were held that proved so popular they were held again the next year. This began the tradition of Oktoberfest.

It is traditional to drink beer at Oktoberfest. In Munich, visitors can stop by the world's largest beer hall, which holds more than eight thousand people. Weihenstephaner, the world's oldest brewery, was founded in Freising, Bavaria, in 1040.

Holidays

All national holidays in Germany are related to the Christian church except for German Unity Day, which is the date that West Germany and East Germany reunited in 1990.

Other holidays celebrated by Germans include St. Nicholas Day, December 6. On this day, children are given bags of candy, which adults get to share.

Fasching, or Karneval, is the carnival season. It begins in November and lasts about three months. Fasching is a time

Public Holidays

New Year's Day	January 1
Epiphany	January 6
Good Friday	March or April
Easter Monday	March or April
Labor Day	May 1
Ascension Day	May or June
Whit Sunday and Monday	May or June
German Unity Day	October 3
Christmas Day	December 25
St. Stephen's Day	December 26

for parties, but it is celebrated in different ways in different parts of Germany. In the northern, Protestant parts, Fasching features fancy balls and parades. In the southern, Catholic regions, especially Bavaria, people wear silly costumes and attend large, outdoor parties.

Weddings and Beyond

Couples planning to get married must give six weeks' notice to the city where they marry. First, the couple has a civil ceremony at city hall to make the marriage legal. It is attended

People dressed as witches take part in a Fasching parade.

Christmas Trees

Evergreen branches have long been used as decorations for celebrations. This was especially true in places that were cold and dark in winter. The Germans were the first people known to decorate with an entire tree. Probably in the sixteenth century, they started bringing evergreen trees into their houses and decorating them. According to legend, Martin Luther had the idea to add candles to the trees. German settlers brought the custom of Christmas trees to North America.

only by a small group of close family and friends. Then on another day a larger, religious ceremony is held in a church. The second ceremony is not required for a couple to be officially married. The city hall ceremony is all that is necessary.

The night before a wedding, friends of the couple break dishes outside the bride's house to bring luck to the marriage.

A popular tradition in Germany that is supposed to bring the bride and groom good luck is called *Polterabend*. That means "racket evening." The night before the wedding, friends of the bride break dishes and throw tin cans on the ground in front of her. Anything noisy is good, except glass, because breaking that is considered bad luck.

In Germany, sausages are often eaten with cabbage.

Great Foods

German meals feature many different kinds of food, but meat and potatoes play a large role. Germany is famous for its sausage. Germans claim to make at least 1,200 kinds. Munich features *weisswurst*, a white veal sausage. Northern Germany has *Kohl und Pinkel*, a dish of curly kale and a special sausage. *Thüringer* is a type of sausage from Thuringia.

Spaetzle is a German noodle that is often served with a meat dish and covered with gravy. It can also be served with cinnamon and butter as a dessert.

In the past, the biggest meal of the day was at noon. Children were home from school and working parents would come home from the job. But with both parents working in most homes now, that is gradually changing. The bigger meal is usually now in the evening.

A Turkish dish called doner kebab is a favorite meal in Germany.

Pretzels

Lots of different baked goods are made from a combination of flour, yeast, and water. But only pretzels are twisted into a lopsided figure 8 before they are baked. No one knows for sure why pretzels have that shape or how the name *pretzel* was invented. They just know that pretzels taste good. Pretzels can be soft, to be eaten right away, or hard, to be kept for a long time. They can have salt on them, or even chocolate. One type of pretzel can be worn on a string around the neck and eaten when and where the wearer wants.

A wide variety of fast foods or take-out meals are available in Germany. People enjoy a Turkish dish called doner kebab. Meat, especially lamb or chicken, is roasted on a vertical spit. The meat is sliced very thin and then put into pita bread. Indian and Chinese take-out are also very popular. American fast-food chains such as McDonald's, Burger King, and KFC are also available.

The hamburger became popular with people traveling through Hamburg, Germany, and the frankfurter sausage originated in Frankfurt. The origin of the word *pumpernickel* isn't known, and there's no town named Pumpernickel, but that delicious dark bread was invented in Westphalia.

Germans have also created many great desserts. Christmas is the time to eat *Lebkuchen* (gingerbread), *Stollen* (sweet bread with fruit), and anise-flavored *Springerle* (a hard cookie great for dunking in milk). When the Christmas tree was introduced into North America, so were Springerle cookies.

Timeline

German History

Otto von Bismarck is named prime minister of Prussia.	1862
Prussia leads the founding of the German Empire.	1871
World War I ends, with Germany declared a republic.	1918
The National Socialist (Nazi) Party, led by Adolf Hitler, gains control of Germany.	1933
Germany invades Poland, starting World War II.	1939
Nazi leaders agree to the "Final Solution," a plan to murder all European Jews.	1942
Germany surrenders, ending World War II in Europe.	1945
The Berlin Airlift begins.	1948
West Germany becomes the Federal Republic of Germany; East Germany becomes the German Democratic Republic.	1949
The Soviet Union builds the Berlin Wall between East and West Berlin.	1961
The Berlin Wall is torn down; communism falls in Eastern Europe.	1989
East Germany and West Germany are reunited.	1990
The European Union is formed.	1992
The euro replaces the deutsche mark as Germany's currency.	2002
Angela Merkel becomes the first East German and first woman chancellor.	2005
Germany works to stabilize currency in the Eurozone.	2012

World History

1865	The American Civil War ends.
1879	The first practical lightbulb is invented.
1914	World War I begins.
1917	The Bolshevik Revolution brings communism to Russia.
1929	A worldwide economic depression begins.
1939	World War II begins.
1945	World War II ends.
1969	Humans land on the Moon.
1975	The Vietnam War ends.
1989	The Berlin Wall is torn down as communism crumbles in Eastern Europe.
1991	The Soviet Union breaks into separate states.
2001	Terrorists attack the World Trade Center in New York City and the Pentagon near Washington, D.C.
2004	A tsunami in the Indian Ocean destroys coastlines in Africa, India, and Southeast Asia.
2008	The United States elects its first African American president.

Fast Facts

Official name: Federal Republic of Germany

Capital: Berlin

Official language: German

Munich

German flag

Rhine River

Official religion:	None
National anthem:	"Deutschlandlied" ("Song of Germany")
Type of government:	Federal republic
Head of state:	President
Head of government:	Chancellor
Area of country:	137,846 square miles (357,000 sq km)
Greatest distance north to south:	540 miles (870 km)
Greatest distance east to west:	390 miles (628 km)
Bordering countries:	Denmark to the north; Poland and the Czech Republic to the east; Austria and Switzerland to the south; France, Luxembourg, Belgium, and the Netherlands to the west
Highest elevation:	Zugspitze, 9,717 feet (2,962 m) above sea level
Lowest elevation:	In Neuendorf bei Wilster, Schleswig-Holstein, 11.6 feet (3.5 m) below sea level
Average high temperature:	In Berlin, 75°F (24°C) in July; 37°F (3°C) in January
Average annual precipitation:	20 to 28 inches (51 to 71 cm) in the northern lowlands; 80 inches (203 cm) in the Bavarian Alps

Brandenburg Gate

National population (2011 est.): 81.4 million

Population of major cities (2011 est.):

Berlin	3,439,100
Hamburg	1,769,117
Munich	1,220,440
Cologne	998,105
Frankfurt	695,000

Landmarks:
- ▶ *Black Forest*, Baden-Württemberg
- ▶ *Brandenburg Gate*, Berlin
- ▶ *Cologne Cathedral*, Cologne
- ▶ *Neuschwanstein Castle*, Füssen
- ▶ *Reichstag*, Berlin

Economy: Germany is one of the largest exporting countries in the world. It produces many steel products such as automobiles and machine tools. Other important products include electrical equipment, computers, metals, cameras, clothing, and processed foods. Major agricultural products include wheat, corn, potatoes, sugar beets, rapeseed, and milk.

Currency: The euro. In 2012, €1.00 equaled US$1.25, and US$1.00 equaled €0.80.

System of weights and measures: Metric system

Literacy rate (2006): 99%

Currency

Schoolchildren

Boris Becker

Common German words and phrases:

ja	yes
nein	no
bitte	please; you're welcome
danke	thank you
guten Tag	good day; hello
auf Wiedersehen	good-bye
Wie geht es ihnen?	How are you?
Ich verstehe nicht.	I don't understand.

Prominent Germans:

Johann Sebastian Bach *Composer*	(1685–1750)
Boris Becker *Tennis player*	(1967–)
Ludwig van Beethoven *Composer*	(1770–1827)
Benedict XVI *Pope*	(1927–)
Albert Einstein *Scientist*	(1879–1955)
Hildegard of Bingen *Writer and composer*	(1098–1179)
Adolf Hitler *Dictator, chancellor*	(1889–1945)
Angela Merkel *Chancellor*	(1954–)

To Find Out More

Books

▶ Mills, Clifford W. *Angela Merkel*. Philadelphia: Chelsea House Publishers, 2008.

▶ Stein, R. Conrad. *World War II*. New York: Children's Press, 2012.

▶ Watts, Irene H., and Kathryn E. Shoemaker. *Good-bye Marianne: A Story of Growing Up in Nazi Germany*. New York: Tundra Books, 2008.

Music

▶ Brahms, Johannes. *A German Requiem*. Chicago Symphony Orchestra. Berlin: Deutsche Grammophon, 2005.

▶ *The World's a Stage: Music of Oktoberfest*. New York: Sheridan Square, 2007.

▶ Visit this Scholastic Web site for more information on Germany:
www.factsfornow.scholastic.com
Enter the keyword **Germany**

Index

Page numbers in *italics* indicate illustrations.

Meet the Author

A LOVER OF CATS, THE INTERNET, CHILDREN, EUROPE, travel, books, sunshine, and much, much more, Jean F. Blashfield most of all delights in sharing what she enjoys with other people. One way she does this is by writing books on her favorite subjects.

Sometimes, she says, her biggest problem is figuring out what to leave out of a book because she becomes so fascinated by every bit of information. The problem of what to leave out was especially true for a book on Germany, because many of her friends are of German ancestry and some go back there often to see relatives. They all have stories about Germany and would say, "Did you include this?" and "Don't forget about…!"

Blashfield first visited Germany on a college choir tour. She was so enchanted by everything she saw that she made up her mind that she would go back. After developing the *Young People's Science Encyclopedia* for Children's Press, she kept that promise to herself. She made a long, slow journey the length of Germany, from Denmark to Switzerland.

Since then, she has returned to Germany often (but not often enough! she says). Lately, she's been amazed and intrigued at the changes that have taken place since she first started going there when it was still in its postwar desolation, but beautiful nonetheless. It recent times, it has become an exciting, forward-looking country.

Jean Blashfield has written more than 160 books, most of them for young people. Many of them have been for Scholastic's Enchantment of the World and America the Beautiful series. She has also created an encyclopedia of aviation and space, written popular books on murderers and houseplants, and had

a lot of fun creating a book on the things women have done, called *Hellraisers, Heroines, and Holy Women*. She also founded the Dungeons & Dragons fantasy book department, which is now part of Wizards of the Coast.

Born in Madison, Wisconsin, Jean Blashfield grew up in the Chicago area. She graduated from the University of Michigan and worked for publishers in Chicago, New York, and London, and for NASA in Washington, D.C. She returned to Wisconsin and the Lake Geneva area when she married Wallace Black (a publisher, writer, and pilot) and began to raise a family. She has two grown children, one a professor of medieval history and one who manages an academic department at Stanford University, and three grandchildren.

Photo Credits